First published in the Federal
Republic of Germany 1987
by Ravensburger Buchverlag
First published in Great Britain 1989
by Victor Gollancz Ltd
14 Henrietta Street, London WC2E 8QJ

© 1987 by Ravensburger Buchverlag Otto Maier GmbH
Original German title: *Ich Mach Was Mit Holz*

British Library Cataloguing in Publication Data
Lohf, Sabine
   Things I make with wood
   1. Handicrafts using wood. Manuals. For children
   I. Title
   745.51

ISBN 0-575-04543-4

Printed in the Federal Republic of Germany

Sabine Lohf

Things I make with wood

You can make
all these things
with wood!

LONDON • VICTOR GOLLANCZ LTD • 1989

Putting Bits and Pieces Together

Sticking Bits and Pieces Together

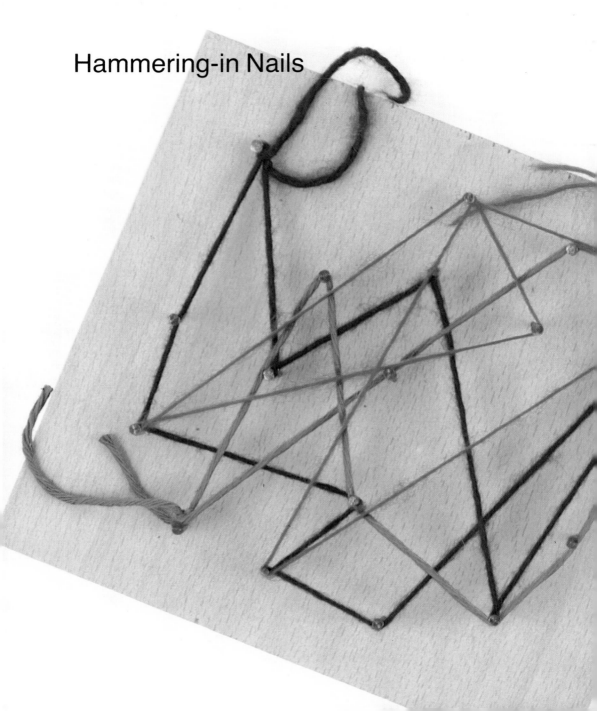

Hammering-in Nails

Making Animals

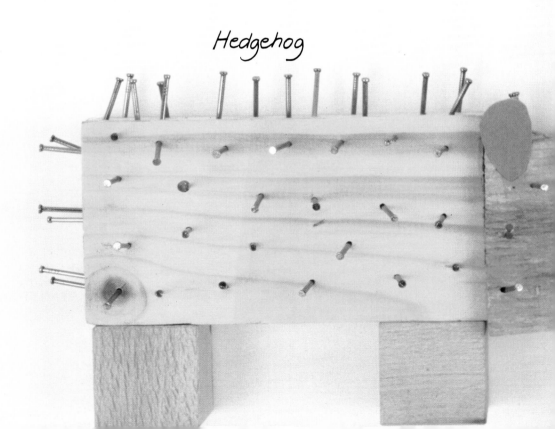

Hedgehog

Centipede

Wooden Boats

Wood floats really well.

A Puzzle

I laid blocks of wood together, and painted a ladybird on them, to make a puzzle.

A Dice Game

Make the dice from small cubes of wood.

Draw squares to make the board, like this. Who will win – blue, green or purple?

Paint faces on the pieces, like this.

Rubber Stamps

Cut pieces of rubber
bands and erasers into
the shapes you want,

then stick them
on small blocks of wood.

Scissor-Beasts

Musical Instruments

You can drum with these.

What sort of music shall I make?

Rubber band zither

Make a rattle with wooden beads.

A Monster

Cut the *monster out of plywood.* The *legs are made from clothes pegs. Your beast will look really fierce if you paint it bright red.*

A Marionette

Fix it together with string and staples.

Would you like a little friend?